Saving

Charlotte

Saving Charlotte

Fumbling Across America with a Reluctant VW Bus

KAT WIECHERT

Afterword by
NED BACON

Heartfelt thanks go out to Charlie and Becky for their gracious hospitality and witty company, and for providing a much appreciated, much needed "safe-house" halfway through our journey.

Many thanks, also, to Lucas, Taylor, and the rest of the Go-Westy gang for helping Charlotte evolve into a healthy and capable traveler.

Table of Contents

Chapter One

The SAMBA Site

Ned has a disease called VW-itis. Ned is the car-crazed guy I share my life with in Northern Nevada, and his affliction can best be described as a compulsion to purchase and own multiple VW vehicles in spite of their notorious unreliability and their need for constant mechanical tinkering. Half of the time Ned's disease is in remission, but the flare-up of spring, 2006 was a bad one. Many late nights spent on The Samba (a Volkswagen focused website) yielded countless possibilities and fanciful ideas about how this DOCA (double cab bus) or that Vanagon 4X4 "Syncro" might be fixed up into a cool off-road, long distance travel vehicle. Every morning Ned would call me over to the computer to examine his "finds" from the previous night.

Ned and I had already experienced many vehicular-based travel adventures together, and had most recently been enjoying our off-the-beaten-path trips in a Toyota Tacoma. A VW for overland travel wasn't seriously on our radar until March of 2006. We were in a remote location in Baja, Mexico, watching the San Felipe 250 off-road race, and the weather was foul. The howling wind and drenching rain kept us vehicle-bound. That was the moment we decided that a VW bus might be the perfect machine for roaming the rugged back roads of Baja, or anywhere else. The hours we spent squished in the tiny cab of the Tacoma inspired dreams of being able to wander comfortably around in a bus with access to food, clothing, and a bed in any weather.

At home, one morning in June, I was enthusiastically summoned to my usual VW viewing. Ned had found a 1987 Syncro Bus with only 31k original miles. This was rare. Volkswagen stopped importing Syncros in 1991 and most of these vehicles now have 200k-300k miles on them. It appears that people love to drive these things and good ones tend to sell for upward of $30k. From the pictures online, this bus looked cherry, sporting shiny burgundy paint and a clean, gray interior.

A phone call to its owner, John, however, uncovered a few "small" issues. First of all, the bus was located 3,000 miles away in Hartford, Connecticut. Then there was a "little" rust on the exhaust pipes and it was a "little" loud. And finally, there was the smashed in right front corner and subsequent "Salvage Title."

Undaunted, we discovered we could fly one-way to Hartford for $135 each. After confirming that John would hold the bus for us until July 25, and making sure we could get a clean title from the Nevada DMV once we repaired the dent, we made the deal, sent John a deposit, and booked our flight.

Without exception, friends and family thought our plan was risky, and they were probably right. We had bought this bus "sight-unseen" with the intention of driving it across the country with no registration and a bashed-in front end. To Ned and me, it seemed like a grand adventure, and we were very excited. Our friends jokingly agreed to post bail if necessary!

On July 24th we caught a red-eye flight to Connecticut. Since we were planning to camp on the drive home, we brought all of our gear, including our large Rubbermaid "cook box," in which we also stowed the all-important automotive tools. The airline, of course, charged us an extra $100 for the 100lb monster, but it was worth it, as having it along would keep us self-sufficient.

We landed in Hartford at 10:00am on Tuesday, July 25 filled with anticipation. Finally, after 6 weeks, answers to the countless questions rattling around in our brains would be revealed. What was the bus really like? How well would it run? What was John like? Would our 100lb cook/tool box make it through the heightened 9/11 security and the flight intact?

Chapter Two

Charlotte

It must have been a good luggage day, because everything made it off of the flight just fine. We scampered out to the passenger pick-up curb, eager to see where this impulsive adventure would take us.

We had made sure ahead of time that John knew we had a lot of luggage, emphasizing the need for him to bring a large vehicle. After connecting via cell phone a couple of times, and being informed that he was driving a VW Passat, we spotted the tiny wagon ambling toward us. We flagged it down, and "mystery man" John pulled up to the curb.

Upon seeing him, the first question that occurred to us was how on earth this guy crammed himself into the driver's seat. He was not a small person, and it appeared that he was hunched over and practically bulging out of the window. The second thing we noticed were the two infant seats in the back, complete with two infants. We looked at each other with an unspoken question of…how the hell are *we* going to fit in this thing, let alone our luggage?

Unabashedly, John heaved himself out of the car, and introduced himself, while flinging open the back hatch and waving away the hay which came flying out. John then removed the spare tire, which was also rolling around in there, and set it on the curb. One small Passat, one large John, 2 babies in infant seats, the two of us, a spare tire, a 100 lb. cook box, and the rest of our bags…hmmm…this was going to be interesting. As we were offering to find alternative transportation, John unceremoniously shouldered his considerable bulk against the cook box and managed to wedge it into the back, all the while apologizing for the kids, and mumbling that he *did* have a friend with a pickup…

Overnight flights typically leave you in a dazed state anyway, and I watched with fascinated detachment as John actually managed to fit almost everything into the back, even the spare tire and stray hay. He then graciously offered me (and my bag) the remaining room in the back seat…all 12 inches of it. Happily I am a small person, so I pressed myself up against the nearest child seat, settled my bag on my lap, and forced the door closed. Then I turned to my left, and gazed into the limitless depth of the most crystalline blue eyes I have ever seen. John was a cherubic-looking man with plump rosy cheeks and very curly red hair. This child staring at me like Gandhi reincarnated was cherubic times five. I asked the little angel what her name was and she sagely answered, "Charlotte," all while continuing to touch my soul with her quiet gaze.

As we endured the hour long trip to John's "house" I kept half of my attention on John, explaining in detail to a fascinated Ned how he had converted this diesel Passat to run on french-fry oil. The rest of my attention was focused on a "conversation" with Charlotte as the vague smell of french-fries wafted around us. I managed to find out that Charlotte was two years old and her sister, Hanna (still sleeping) was one.

We finally arrived at John's "work-in-progress" home. It turned out that John had been working on his unfinished house (complete with the manufacturer's stickers on the windows) for several years while he, his wife, and his kids lived in a 300 sq. ft. shack in the back. I asked Charlotte where her Mommy was, and she wisely said, "She's at work, because Mommy says that EVERYBODY has to work!" It was becoming apparent that Daddy didn't!

Finally we got to see our new bus. John disappeared into his shack, letting us look it over, while Charlotte (now transformed from Gandhi into Little Orphan Annie) ran around the yard, wild and out of control, vying for our attention. Curiously, Hanna was as dull and blank as her sister was bright.

The bus was puzzling too. The body and interior were immaculate, but the engine and exhaust looked like they had been under the ocean for a year. The exhaust had more than just a "little" rust, and the engine was covered in corrosion. If the rest of the vehicle hadn't looked so good we would have thought the thing had been through Hurricane Katrina. John came out of the shack with the vehicle's paperwork and we attempted to decipher its past based on the title records. This bus was quickly becoming our "mystery woman." From what we could see on the title transfer sheets, she had had one (unknown) owner for many years, and was not driven much. Then, in November, 2005 she was acquired by a woman who subsequently wrecked her in March of 2006. The insurance company totaled the now damaged bus and sold her to a salvage company. Fortunately, someone at the wrecking yard realized the value of her low mileage, and sold her to a broker, who sold her to a dealer friend of John's, who sold her to John...all in three weeks. But that still didn't explain the rusty engine and neither did John.

Unfortunately, we also discovered that John's ownership was not listed anywhere in the paperwork. He was extremely flustered when we pointed out this "small" detail, and quickly disappeared into his shack again, presumably to find proof of his ownership. Charlotte started tugging on my hand again, and their dog, some sort of a border collie cross, dropped a ball down the driveway and chased it into the street. This act had to be a death-wish on the dog's part, as the driveway was on a blind corner. As Ned and I worried about the animal's imminent demise, John reappeared and laughed dismissively, saying, "Oh, yeah, that dog has already been hit twice doing that, but, uh, I don't know, for some reason, he just keeps on doing it!" Brilliant.

John then proceeded to tell us that he couldn't find any document showing his ownership, but not to worry, "because possession is nine tenth of the law!" Our frustration mounted as we asked John to call his dealer friend for a duplicate copy, and he defensively and repeatedly said to Ned (calling him "guy"), "Guy, my friend is just not around, this paperwork will be fine!" Any logical, sane person would have walked away at this point, but, of course, we stayed.

In spite of his seemingly hurt feelings and persistently urging "guy" to trust him, John did finally disappear around the corner to call his previously "unavailable" friend. John emerged from his shack yet again, reporting that his friend, the previous owner, had agreed to provide a copy of the title showing John's ownership. But we were still feeling more uneasy by the minute. John's secrecy, his insistence on cash, and the under-the-ocean appearance of the bus, was all adding up to a really fishy deal. And we hadn't even heard the thing run yet.

But here we were in Hartford, with our one-way tickets and our luggage. So what was the next logical step? Start the motor, of course!

Through the billows of ugly black smoke pouring out of the exhaust, I could see Ned's face beginning to show definite signs of anger. The entire exhaust system was rusted down to the head flanges and now there appeared to be internal issues with the engine. Ned then turned on John, informing him that the car had not been advertised accurately and that it would never make it back to Nevada. In response, John turned up the volume on his defensive, hurt puppy look, reached into his pocket and "upchucked" the $500 deposit in cash. He proceeded to peel bank notes off of the wad and shove them into Ned's hand, asking if that was enough to pay for a flight home! Ned pocketed the bills.
It was obviously time for us to make some decisions. In the meantime, the place was still in chaos. John must have offered us sodas about a dozen times, literally shoving the bottles into our hands, while the kids and dog still ran loudly amuck. Then the

grandparents showed up and began playing with the kids…all right there in the midst of our growing confrontation. Ned and I asked for some privacy to talk, and walked around behind the house.

Stranded with our 100lb cook box, we decided to make some phone calls. We rang several relatives in the New England area to see if they could rescue us, but none were available. We also called the airline to see about a flight home, but of course, short notice flights would cost us more than the $6,000 asking price of the bus! After reasoning back and forth, we finally bolstered each other's confidence and felt back in control. We approached John with three options: 1. A $4,000 offer for the bus; 2. We take it in to the VW dealer to have it fixed, and he pays for it, or 3. He drives us back to the airport.

Without blinking, John said, "Get in the Passat, it's worth $15,000!" So much for being in control.

By this time, the bus had been idling for a while and the black smoke had cleared up a bit. Absurdly, we figured we might as well try to drive the dumb thing, and much sobered by John's refusal to succumb to our impressive negotiating skills, we mentioned this to him. John brightened instantly and jumped in the driver's seat, not offering to let Ned drive. Resigned, we shrugged to each other and climbed in. We were surprised and pleased when the bus ran perfectly for John.

Upon arriving back at the house, however, we let the engine idle for a while and it started sounding very bad again. Our "mystery woman" was fast becoming less intriguing and more exasperating, but some small voice (maybe hers!) must have been whispering in our ears to buy her anyway. And so began the embarrassing process of groveling. We offered $5,000, as is; John refused. We offered $5,500; John sat on his hands.

Okay, maybe it was time for Ned to actually drive the damn thing. Unbelievably, we had to force the issue, but we finally climbed in with Ned behind the wheel. Since the gauge read empty, we drove to a gas station where Ned generously paid for some fuel and put air in the tires. The bus had a short bout of sputtering and lurching, but otherwise Ned was impressed, and said that it felt very tight, like it really did only have 31k miles on it. Finally, knowing we were nuts, we agreed to pay the full $6,000.

With the incomplete paperwork, a bill of sale (from a person not listed as an owner), the name and address of the "dealer friend," and a promise to send the correct transfer of title, we took possession of our new bus. Unenthusiastically waving to John, Charlotte and Hanna, we drove away in an unlicensed car that we did not legally own, complete with a bashed in front end, a badly cracked windshield, and a headlight propped in with duct tape, a tree branch and a piece of foam found lying on the ground. It was not an encouraging way to start our 3,000 mile journey!

A bashed-in front end and a "salvage title." Not a promising way to start our 3,000 mile journey!

Chapter Three

Can't Get Out of Hartford

Hungry and exhausted from lack of sleep and the four-hour ordeal with John, we felt a little numb, but were still cautiously excited, grinning at each other with child-like anticipation. We were anxious to be on the road in our new bus, dreamily picturing all of those great travel adventures we would have in it. Our giddy excitement, however, quickly turned into stomach-sinking anxiety as the bus started lurching and coughing just a half mile from John's driveway.

Sitting quietly in the passenger seat, I grimaced inside, but outwardly remained confident. I always tease Ned, saying, "You can fix anything!" Ned is competent and resourceful, and knowing this helps me stay calm and in good humor despite the many challenges that can come with vehicular travel. I have sat many times in the "middle of nowhere," reading, while complicated mechanical and electrical problems get handled. But in this case, I was very pleased when Ned's good common sense prompted him to say, "Let's eat."

John had recommended a "famous" restaurant called Rein's Deli, so we limped and lurched our way down the road and into the deli parking lot. I don't think our opinion was very objective at the time, but, famished, we both thought the food was the best we had ever eaten!

Now bolstered by nourishment and our natural optimism, we headed north from Hartford on the I-91 toward the Massachusetts border. Over dinner we had discussed a name for our new baby and settled on "Gustine," (feminine for the old Bay Window VW bus I used to own named "Gus the Bus"). Unfortunately, Gustine seemed a little reluctant to leave Hartford, running so badly that we had to pull over. Ned suspected a problem with the fuel injection, but admitted to having no experience with the idiosyncrasies of Vanagon fuel system quirks. With night approaching, coupled with the day's trials, he was feeling a bit defeated.

During our "negotiations" with John, he had mentioned a guy named Tom who was a mechanic at the VW dealership in town. So, feeling like fools, we limped back down the highway to Hartford proper to get a diagnosis.

The repair shop was closed, of course, and Tom had left for the day. But we met one of the salesmen named Scott who was very kind and helpful. Desperately wanting to get out of Hartford, we mentioned to Scott that we had been told Tom might do some after hours work at home. Scott kind of chuckled and told us with a shrug that, "Tom likes to go right home after work and drink beer. He's probably a little looped by now!" But he urged us to stay the night, letting us know that the service manager was a great guy and would take care of us first thing in the morning.

Having nothing better to do for the evening, we made the first of what would turn out to be many forays into the Walmarts and Home Depots abundantly littered across the country. We wandered around for a couple of hours, contemplating just how we were going to fix up the newest member of our fleet. Finally, completely bored we made a couple of calls and booked a (very) cheap motel room. With everything else that had gone on, this was by far the most discouraging part of the day. We had brought that 100lb cook box with all of our gear so we could do a cross-country camping trip, not a flea-bitten motel trip!

Our cheap motel room turned out to be on the other end of town, of course, and we worried about drawing attention to our illegally unlicensed vehicle. Ned is a journalist who writes for several off-road magazines, and had cleverly put a Four Wheeler Magazine "license plate" on the rear (where a legal one should have been!). This was only a small comfort as Gustine coughed loudly, spewed black smoke, and jerked violently while we "snuck" our way back onto the freeway. To make matters worse, our jerry-rigged headlight began to droop in the most obvious way. Feeling slightly stressed by now (can you believe we haven't had one argument yet?) we missed our exit, racking up even more agonizing highway miles and inviting the attention of Hartford's finest.

We did eventually make it safely to our $48.95 EconoLodge room. In spite of the filth-encrusted carpet which covered the rotting floorboards, we had a good night's sleep and a hot shower and were ready for day two of our grand adventure.

Our New VW Bus sporting her Four Wheeler Magazine "license plate."

Not surprisingly, the bus ran perfectly all the way back to the VW dealership the next morning. Also not surprising was that the wonderful service manager, John, was not in. In his place, we had the unfortunate experience of dealing with Jeff, a "Nazi-Worm" of a man who would not promise anything, but "might" be able to have "someone" look at the bus "sometime" today, and would not let us speak to the mechanic, Tom.

Our new friend, Scott, sympathetically sent us up the street to the local diner. This turned out to be a Thai Restaurant, with signs plastered across the front advertising "American Breakfast." The food actually turned out to be good, and we were further surprised to find our bus already on a lift in the service bay when we wandered back. We were also pleased to find out that it was Tom doing the diagnostic work, and Ned, wanting to be in control, of course, kept going into the service bay to discuss the progress with him. This ruffled the feathers of our manager buddy, Jeff, and I still laugh every time I think of him chasing Ned off like a cackling, protective hen. Undaunted, Ned kept going back with Jeff running him off at least a half-dozen times.

Two hours and $185 later, we were back on the road. Tom had changed some ground wires, and told us everything was fine now. We needed to get gas, but just before pulling into a station, we spotted a cop. We quickly ducked into an office complex parking lot to wait for "the coast to clear!" At the time, I was 46 and Ned was 48, so this antic made us both feel a bit childish. We sheepishly grinned at each other as we crept back out and onto I-91 (again!).

As much as we wanted out of Hartford, Gustine started dragging her tires again. Same problem, same symptoms. We lurched and sputtered to the shoulder of the freeway and called our VW Dealership "friends" again who told us to "Come on back in. Can't promise anything, but we'll try to get it back in the service bay sometime today!" Ugghhhh....Massachusetts was dead ahead, and we just couldn't go back to Hartford!

14

By this point, it was apparent that this little journey might be worth documenting, but neither of us had thought to bring a camera. So we pulled into another gas station, bought beer, ice and some cheap disposable cameras (basic necessities) and headed for the Massachusetts border, agreeing that we would "just deal with it!"

We finally left Hartford behind and crossed the state line into Massachusetts. We never dreamed we would have such an adventure, so we had left our good cameras at home. After the first day it became apparent that this trip would need some documentation! Kat is pictured in the mirror with one of our super hi-tech disposable cameras.

We limped onward, and discovered that if we pulled over to let the bus rest every 20 miles or so, she would run fine for a while. Further thought led Ned to the theory that large pieces of debris were in the gas tank and settling over the screen as gas was being pumped into the engine. So Ned, still not wanting to draw attention to ourselves, would weave violently every once in a while to "dislodge" the sediment. This seemed to work pretty well, and between that and pulling over, we finally managed to stagger our way out of Connecticut and into Massachusetts.

We made it all the way into New York and on to Niagara Falls, and even had one stretch of 125 problem-free miles. We had brought along a Mark Knoffler and Emmylou Harris CD, and one of the lines in a song about life on the road became our theme for the rest of the trip:

> Rollin' on, rollin' on
> Feeling better than we did last night
> Rollin' on, rollin' on
> It's hard sometimes, but pretty much it's alright

We put Hartford behind us, wondering if Gustine was starting to get over her fear and was settling into the idea of going west!

Chapter Four

Not Gustine, Charlotte!

Our plan was to go see Niagara Falls since I had never been there, and then, since it was Niagara Falls, we assumed there would be some nice choices for dinner. We would then head south to find somewhere to pull over and camp. Ned had been to the falls once before on the Canadian side of the river, and had eaten in a very nice restaurant. The falls were impressive and well worth seeing, but the town (on the American side) was a small, sad version of Coney Island. There was nothing to eat but corn dogs and potato chips! We were starving again, and stared, drooling, across the raging waters to the nice Canadian side with all of those great restaurants. It would have been a simple matter of just crossing the river/border, but the reality of our unlicensed vehicle made it a frustrating impossibility.

Resigned, we crawled into the back of the bus, opened a couple of beers, and just relaxed with the sliding door and all of the windows open. The weather was perfect, and a deep sense of contentment came over both of us as we clinked our beer bottles together, praising the benefits of "bus living!" It really was nice having a car like this to travel and hang out in. At this point it was still a seven-passenger van and had two rows of back seats. Our halfway stop on the trip would be Ned's cousin's home in Minneapolis, Minnesota, and there, we intended to get rid of the seats and build a bed, so we would have a "camper."

But there, sprawled out on the two back seats, happily sipping our beer, we started really contemplating our bus' past. From what history we could piece together, she had led quite the sheltered life, probably kept in a garage, driven very little, and had not been exposed to the harsh climate of the East Coast. Then, in the fall of 2005, she was sold to the woman who ended up crashing her (probably into a snow bank). That was when the insurance company declared her totaled and how she ended up in our hands. The rust on the exhaust obviously happened that first winter of 2005, 2006 when she was cruelly thrown into a cold, wet environment with no garage, and plenty of salted roads.

By now the beer (on our empty stomachs) was feeling pretty good, and our fancy led to more speculation. The bus had obvious reasons to be reluctant to head west, having led such a sheltered life for her first 18 years. She was after, all, a city girl, and life had not been kind over the last six months. But the bus was starting to endear herself to us, and we imagined that we were rescuing her. It was also there, going over the events and the people that had led us to this point, that our red bus' real name became clear. We would call her "Charlotte," a cherubic-faced Gandhi reminder to always strive for wisdom, but to stay young at heart.

Niagara Falls

Chapter Five

Can't Get Out of Buffalo

By the time we quit our musings and started paying attention to our growling stomachs, it was around 8:30pm. It was still Wednesday, day two of our trip, and we were tired and hungry (again!). Still slightly buzzed from the beer, we drove through the town of Buffalo looking for a decent restaurant. What we found was an urban hell. We managed to hit every red traffic light in a neighborhood where you'd really rather not have to stop at all. The streets were dirty and deserted, and most of the buildings were boarded up; the kind of neighborhood where windows and doors are dismally clad in iron security bars.

At one point, while still on the freeway, we had spotted a nice looking restaurant sign that read "Harry's." We were certainly not going to find anything where we were, so we made our way back onto the freeway to try to find "Harry's." An aggravating 30 minutes later, we pulled into "Harry's" parking lot, climbed wearily out of the bus, and into the elegant foyer of a Five-Star restaurant. We just looked at each other and started laughing. We were road worn and rumpled, and since we were wearing some of our finest "grubbies," we probably looked like homeless people. Add to that that the cheapest item on the menu was a $28 hamburger, and we fled in shame before the maitre d' could spot us.

By now, it was starting to rain, and Charlotte was hungry too. We found the one gas station that was open in this dreary place. It was a full service station, so the "gas jockey" took our debit card, and filled the tank. I happened to spot a little sandwich shop called Tim Horton's across the street, so I scampered over to see if they were still open. With a great sigh of relief, I walked in and started looking over the menu. Unfortunately, it was closing time, and the staff had locked the doors behind me. By the time Ned got there, he could not get in. The friendly, helpful staff agreed to feed *me*, but not Ned, since *he* had *not* gotten there *before* the sacred closing time. Fortunately, they did agree to unlock the door so I could get out.

We had been traveling south on the 1-90, but on our way up to Niagara Falls on the 290, we had noticed a Texas Roadhouse restaurant in a nice, well-lit, modern, "box-store-ish" part of town. At this point, it seemed like a great idea to backtrack and get some food.

Miraculously, we made it just under the wire...it was 10pm and they locked the doors behind (both of) us. The crew was great, the food was wonderful, and so it made perfect sense to finally have an argument. The topic was ridiculous, of course, and between glares, Ned reached for his wallet and discovered his debit card was missing. The nice gas station attendant had failed to return it. Ok, argument forgotten, now we have better things to worry about. We drove the 20 minutes back to the gas station only to find it closed.

We called the emergency number posted on the kiosk. A fellow named Peter, who turned out to be in Pennsylvania, took our call. Evidently this was a chain of 300 gas stations, and we had reached their "security" department. We patiently (yeah right) explained the situation to Peter, who told us to stay put and wait for a call from "Larry." Meanwhile, we were quite obvious, sitting there in a nicely lit, but closed gas station, so Ned strategically parked Charlotte with her bashed-in side facing away from any patrolling police officers. We were anxiously waiting for our phone call, when the inevitable cop did drive up and asked what we were doing there. Ned cleverly diverted his attention away from our missing license plate by walking up to his car and dramatically describing our plight. The officer obviously had more serious matters to attend to there in Buffalo, so he shrugged, told us good luck, and drove away.

The phone finally rang, but it was some recorded message…in Spanish! Was that Larry???? What were we supposed to do now? We were just about to our maximum frustration level, when Larry actually did call. The other call was some random coincidence. Larry told us to come back to the gas station at 6am when it re-opened to get our card. Nobody could help us tonight. We were stuck in Buffalo.

We made the decision to go back to the bright lights of the Texas Roadhouse area. Surely there would be a good motel in that neighborhood. But by now it was raining…hard, and even Charlotte got crabby and started acting like she did not want to leave again. She was smoking and coughing, and we had to pull over three times. There were no motels to be found, and we had to continue on down a side road for another 30 minutes, certain that we would be noticed and pulled over by one of the many cops we saw. And of course, we hit every red light along the way, cringing each time, hoping Charlotte would stay running.

Then, like a beacon from heaven, a "Microtel" sign blazed through the rain. Unfortunately, it took us another 15 minutes to navigate our way around the curbs and gutters to get into the place. We eventually did rent a room, but stood soaking in the rain while trying and failing to get the key to work. It was 1:00am when we finally fell, exhausted, into bed.

Thursday morning. Day three. We woke up long enough to call the gas station at 6am. The guy did have our card, so we energetically went back to sleep.

At 10am we recovered our wayward debit card and headed south on Hwy 5. This turned out to be our first experience with east coast toll roads. We're from Nevada. We don't have toll roads. We got frustrated and decided to take a side road where we eventually stopped to get ice and groceries (good idea). Now the traffic lights were driving us crazy, so we went back to the lesser evil of the toll roads. Charlotte was running badly again, too, so Ned got the brilliant idea that there must be a vacuum issue with the fuel delivery. He removed the gas cap and she ran 450 miles without a hitch.

Chapter Six

Can't Get Out of Elkhart

We were heading west now, on I-90, breezing through Pennsylvania and Ohio, when the real rain started. This turned out to be a record-breaking torrential storm that was covered by every national news station. Lightning crackled dramatically overhead, and the visibility went to about zero. The other drivers were either pulled over on the side of the road, or going about 10 mph. Ned and Charlotte took the only opportunity we would ever have to pass people! VW buses are not known for speed, and we got a good laugh at the ridiculousness of the situation.

At the next fuel stop, we decided that there was probably enough water in the gas tank, so after filling up, we used some plastic and duct tape to partially cover the exposed opening. We did not want to invite trouble by putting the gas cap back on.

Highway 90 was dreary and monotonously tree-lined. Mile after boring mile of that monochrome green tunnel left us numb. There were no vistas, and no change of scenery. Out west, we take scenery for granted. We're used to the wide-open sky of the desert and spectacular mountains. The East Coast gave us both what we jokingly called "green-tree fever," and we were eager to get to the other side of the Mississippi River.

How we kept water (not!) out of the tank after removing the gas cap.

It seems that once you are on a toll road, there is no escape. The only places to pull over are "service plazas" where you can get gas and eat (or is that, eat and then get gas!). Well, of course it is all fast food, and our dinner that night was memorable only in that it was really, really bad, even by fast food standards. Ned had a coagulated burger, fake pie, and a Dr. Pepper from Burger King, and I had two, two-day-old chicken thighs and wilted coleslaw from KFC. We did take the time to make some calls, and booked a room for the night at a Days Inn. It turned out that we had landed in Elkhart, Indiana, and the clerk at the motel was very cheery. She also proclaimed herself to be "directionally challenged," but we took directions from her anyway, got some fuel, and headed back west on the I-90.

After a number of miles in the still pouring rain, we realized we were heading away from Elkhart. The clerk had sent us in the wrong direction, and we were stuck on the toll road. You cannot exit without paying the toll, so, with limited visibility in the rain, Ned started looking for a place to make an illegal U-turn on the toll road. He grinned at me, saying, "This is when a cop will show up!" We finally passed a connector road, and I sat quietly while he proceeded to pull over to the left shoulder and back up to it. Suddenly, from behind us, we heard, "Rrrnnnnnggg!!!!" The siren didn't necessarily surprise us, but we still managed a simultaneous, "Shit!" This could be the end of the road for us. Our friend Leonard had said that if we made it past the Tetons and needed help, he would come get us with a trailer, but we were still too far east to take him up on the offer. The cop pulled up next to us just before we made the U-turn, and, yelling out his window in the rain, demanded, "What are you doing?!" Ned did his best impression of an idiot tourist, stammering out, "We're looking for exit 96; are we too far west?" The officer rolled his eyes and said, "Yes, but you have to go all the way up to the next exit (7 miles away) in order to turn around. If you make this U-turn here, I'll give you a ticket!" We dreaded pulling out in front of his car for fear of him noticing our Four Wheeler plate, but nothing happened, and we realized the driving rain had saved us. It probably kept the cop in his warm, dry car, when he otherwise would have come up and asked for our license and registration.

Seven miles later, we paid our toll and got off the highway at Exit 83. We decided to take the county roads back to avoid trouble, but still managed to pass all five units of Elkhart's police force. Fortunately they were busy handling challenges brought on by the ferocious storm and paid us no heed. We made it to the Days Inn and met our "directionally challenged" desk clerk, who really was sweet. That night, we made it to bed by 11:00pm.

We heralded Friday, day four, with a refreshed and optimistic 8:00am start. We would put Elkhart behind us today, and make it up to Charlie and Becky's place in Minneapolis in time for dinner!

The freeway entrance was only a block away, but half way up the ramp, Charlotte balked again, fussing so much, that Ned had to conspicuously back down the ramp against traffic. There was a Menard's between the motel and the freeway, so we slipped into the parking lot and pulled over as far away from the store as possible. I kept calling the store May-nard's and Ned was laughing at me, while he crawled under the bus. He knew the problem this time was water in the tank, and he drained the fuel filter while I took a mini jog around the building. We then wandered into Menard's and bought two hose clamps for $1.60. The teenaged, freckle-faced clerk at the register joked with us, saying, "It cost you more in gas to get here than what you just spent here!" Ironically, it was even worse than he figured, since Ned had also just drained out about 6 bucks worth of gasoline in their parking lot, trying to get rid of some water.

After several test laps around the parking lot, Charlotte was still refusing to drink water. We drained a couple more gallons, and she decided to behave. We then made the wise decision to go back into Menard's to buy a fire extinguisher before taking off again.

We drove 10 miles west before Charlotte started lurching again. We pulled off at the next exit, and groaned as we recognized the infamous Exit 83 from last night. We were going in circles.

We wound up in a "Share Ride" parking area and drained off another 10 gallons of gas in the weeds. It wasn't until we were leaving, that we noticed the "Closed for Maintenance" sign. And while I was not proud of our heinous acts of environmental debauchery, I couldn't resist a moment of shared black humor, muttering under my breath, "After our 10 gallons of gas, they're going to need a little more!"

We had some T-shirts made last Christmas that picture a cartoon black sheep, with "Baaaad" written under it. That's on the fronts of the shirts. The backs have the same black sheep with the words, "Doesn't play well with others" over it, and "Questions Authority" below it. Appropriately, Ned was wearing his.

It turned out that we were actually in the neighborhood of Notre Dame College, and passed the famous school on our way to the nearest gas station to fill our now nearly empty tank.

The weather continued to make national news as an unprecedented heat wave settled in to torment the area on the heels of the brutal thunderstorms. It was widespread enough to affect the whole country, but the Midwest got hit the hardest. It was then that we got caught in Chicago's infamous rush-hour traffic. It had failed to be an issue up until this point, but it was now noteworthy that Charlotte has no air conditioning. We call ourselves "desert rats" because we love our arid climate. The high humidity combined with the record breaking 100 plus degree heat hit us pretty hard, as we sat in traffic and long toll lines with no air moving whatsoever.

I had been reading a wonderful novel about Alexander the Great to Ned for most of the drive, and it, at least helped take our minds off of the oppressive heat and our sweaty, sticky selves.

We had approached Chicago at 1:00pm and we paid our final toll at 3:03pm. It had taken us two tortuous hours and a half a dozen tolls to get through the city on what the signs kept calling "The *Real* Expressway." The marquee on the last tollbooth cheerily flashed, "Have a great weekend!"

The Chicago skyline in over 100 degree heat and 90% humidity.

Chapter Seven

Out of Hell

Once past Chicago, the road opened up and became quite scenic. We loved Wisconsin's rolling green hills, and the pristine beauty of its many tidy farms. All of the buildings were clean and well maintained, the fences were painted, and the livestock was glossy and well cared for. There weren't even any backyard junk piles like you find in the rest of rural America. We were starting to relax a little, and even Charlotte was losing her reluctance. She was running uncannily well, and getting better and better gas mileage too. In the beginning it was 14.7mpg, then 17, then 20, and now a whopping 22mpg! It felt weirdly supernatural, as if our princess really was dragging her wheels less and less as she began to get used to us and to being out on the open road.

We crossed the Mighty Mississippi at the Minnesota border and drove into a little rest area along the river. With the East Coast behind us and Charlotte running well, our spirits began to lift. We called Charlie and Becky to let them know that we would make it, but not in time for dinner. Charlie kindly assured us that he would feed us no matter what time we arrived.

In the meantime, we decided to take advantage of this relaxing rest area. We turned up the music, opened a couple of beers and congratulated ourselves for making it this far. The only remaining discomfort was our wrung-out, un-showered, sweaty selves. We playfully looked at each other, then at the mud colored river….well, why not? It was water, wasn't it? At that point, any water sounded refreshing, and nothing could be worse than the way we already felt. Looking forward to the cooling plunge, I still chickened out and made Ned go first. He walked out to the end of a small pier to make sure the water was deep enough, as we could not see the bottom. Without hesitation, Ned took a (thankfully) shallow dive, and wound up belly/face first in what was really two feet of slimy mud! He came up spitting and looking like the "swamp-thing" while I laughed smugly on the shore. *I* sure wasn't getting into *that* muck!

Unfortunately, Ned and I have a pact. If one of us gets into a body of water, no matter where we are, or how cold it is, the other one has to follow. I was vehemently refusing to honor that particular pact, and wondering whose idiot idea it was in the first place, when Ned threatened to throw me in. Since he is bigger than me, and would not hesitate to follow through on the threat, I agreed to go in on my own. Ughhh. I took off my shorts, and in my underwear and a jog-bra, minced my way into the ooze with Ned taunting me the whole time. When I finally whined and squealed my way into about two feet of mud (ick!) topped by six inches of filthy water, I dipped my torso into the gooey mess for about a tenth of a second and then lept back to shore like a wet cat. There, I got in! Now were both covered in smelly mud, but at least I didn't have it in my hair like Ned did! We laughed and drank another beer.

"Swamp Thing" grinning as he emerges from the
Mississippi mud. The slime came all the way up to
above his knees!

Ick! Who made up that stupid pact!

After our mud bath, we headed north on the scenic Hwy 61, which follows the west bank of the Mississippi. The river was wide enough here to look like a lake, and the low sun set the muddy water on fire as it dipped toward the horizon. A train rumbled along on the far shore, and Led Zeppelin came on the X/M radio, playing "Ramble On." Life was good.

Hot, sweaty, grimy, and slimy…but happily headed for Charlie and Becky's place in Minneapolis.

It took us 1600 miles, four days and a twelve-pack each to get to Minneapolis; 1600 miles of staring out of a cracked windshield; 1600 miles of "green tree fever," torrential rain storms, oppressive heat, dodging cops, and nursing Charlotte. But we did finally make it to Ned's cousin's home by 11pm that same Friday.

Never having met Charlie and Becky, I experienced some minor mortification over my state of dishabille. Between the grubby clothes, the road grime, the sweat, and the Mississippi swamp water, I felt disgusting. Ned was no better, but he is their cousin, and they expect it of him!

As I came to find out, though, Charlie and Becky are nothing short of amazing. They are loving and gracious, and have a wonderful

---

sense of humor. Before we could even apologize for ourselves, Charlie hugged me and laughed warmly, saying, "You're sticky!" He then proceeded to feed us an amazing meal at 11pm, and I knew right there, we would be great friends.

The "Twin Cities" were not immune to the heat wave that had laid siege to the country, and Minneapolis was enduring record temperatures of over 100 degrees and 90% plus humidity. We found out that they had not seen triple digits in 11 years. Nonetheless, this became our home away from home for 3 days. Becky called it "Command Central," we called it our safe house. Their beautiful three-story home gave us the opportunity to regroup and refresh before setting out on the next half of our journey.

In spite of the heat, our time in Minneapolis was very productive. We did our laundry, removed the carpeting and the two bench seats from the bus, and scrubbed out the interior. We also made our second trip to a Home Depot where we spent two blissfully air-conditioned hours picking out new carpeting and engineering and purchasing materials for our bed. Charlie and Becky marveled at our perseverance, providing cheerleading services as we sweated our way through the process of re-carpeting and bed construction in their driveway. Becky even managed to produce some sheets and an old foam mattress from their basement that worked perfectly.

Charlotte getting a make-over in Charlie and Becky's driveway. We removed the two bench seats, washed and re-carpeted the interior, built a nice queen-size bed, and installed the foam mattress that Becky had dug out of their basement.

Somewhere along the line, Becky also made a series of phone calls to find a new owner for Charlotte's seats, as they were now excess baggage. She managed to locate a friend of her brother's who ran what turned out to be a questionable VW shop out of his home. He agreed to take the seats, and Ned and I drove Charlotte out to deliver them. He gave us a somewhat laconic greeting when he finally emerged from his hovel, and Ned tried to chat with him, "car guy to car guy," but Bill was a man of few words. We never even got a "thank you," just a small, crooked-toothed smile, and a place to leave the pesky seats.

Our visit with Charlie and Becky turned out to be a highlight of the trip. Their keen intellect and worldly knowledge provided hours of witty, entertaining conversation, and Becky's colorful way with words kept me eager to hear what she would come up with next.

"Bill" didn't say much, but we just knew he was thrilled with his new furniture.

Our timing also coincided with Becky's commitment to help a friend move across town, and playing the part of the perfectly grateful guests, we offered to help. Sunday arrived bearing a temperature of 101 degrees and over 90% humidity. It was moving day! Anita lived in an old apartment from which we hauled her stuff down four flights of narrow, treacherous, non air-conditioned steps. We filled up three vehicles, which took about a dozen trips up and down the stairs, and then drove them over to the new apartment. Anita told us that the new place was a "cake walk," as we only had to endure two flights of stairs!

By the time we unloaded the vehicles and dumped her things unceremoniously on her new floor, we had sweat out about three quarts of water, and decided to go back to the house to continue Charlotte's transformation. Poor Charlie and Becky dragged themselves home late in the afternoon after enduring six more agonizing loads. Henceforth Becky referred to the day as, "The Death March."

Charlie and Becky's delightful daughter, Lucy, came for a visit that night, and, finding us all completely wrung out from the day's ordeal, cheerfully suggested we all go to Matt's Bar for some

"Squirting Burgers." Okay, she had our attention. "What's a Squirting Burger?" Lucy laughed and said we would have to go and find out. We all piled in Becky's Audi, but the battery was dead. Ned and Charlotte came quickly to the rescue with jumper cables, and got the thing running in mere moments. In the meantime, Becky had warned us that Matt's Bar was not a place for "heightened sensibilities," but did have great burgers. It sounded perfect, and turned out to be even better than we expected.

Matt's was a genuine "dive" bar. It was crowded, noisy, dark, and more that a little frayed around the edges. Upon entering, I noticed an intriguing sign proudly posted on the wall proclaiming, "No ice, no plates, we blew our budget on napkins!" The burgers were actually called (coincidently) "Juicy Lucys," and in ravenous self-indulgence, we ordered two each. The Juicy Lucys turned out to be two burger patties pressed together with a slice of American cheese in between, and showed up bubbling hot, thick, and very juicy. True to their nickname, the first bite produced a startling geyser of melted cheesy, greasy burger drippings which arched dramatically toward your nearest table companion. It was hilarious watching the phenomenon occur around the table as we each sank our teeth into our "squirting burgers." To top it off, the sign was absolutely correct. Our burgers came wrapped in paper, the fries came in plastic baskets lined with paper, and the water had no ice. But the beer was cold and they cheerfully provided plenty of napkins for our greasy chins. It was a wonderful evening.

Charlie is an artist, and our plan was to visit his studio in town before heading out. We climbed into the Audi only to find that the battery was dead again. Ned ended up changing the obviously worn out battery and a burnt out light bulb, so Becky, in her wonderful way, christened Ned "The Car Whisperer."

Charlie's art was amazing. He works with both photography and paint, and was currently working on oils of the Badlands National

Park area. He had been spending a lot of time there painting and collecting soil samples for his true to life colors, and his brilliant work brought to life inspiring vistas of striated mountains and endless grasslands. While there at his studio, Charlie helped us plan our trip back home, including stops at the Badlands and Grand Tetons National Parks.

We were looking forward to the open road again, and got a nice alpine start at 2:00pm on Monday, day seven. Charlie and Becky had provided unforgettable hospitality, great memories, and a fine double bed in an upstairs room. Unfortunately Ned is too big to share a double bed and made matters worse by sprawling out cross-ways. This was way too close quarters for the kind of heat that persisted throughout the night, and there were moments when the hardwood floor looked more appealing. Open air and Charlotte's new, comfy, roomy, queen sized bed sounded heavenly. And we would finally be camping.

Chapter Eight

Madelia

It was 102 degrees as we drove down Hwy 169 out of Minneapolis, and, in spite of having opened every window in the bus, the high humidity had us dripping endless rivulets of sweat. It was even worse than Chicago. We suffered for about an hour and a half before spotting another Walmart haven while driving through the town of Mankato. By now Charlotte was well trained to seek out Walmarts and just seemed to pull off the exit without any prompting. Prior to this trip, neither Ned nor I had spent much time in WalMarts, and laughed at ourselves for our easy acceptance of their convenience, selection and great prices! But really, where else could we have enjoyed two hours of blissful air conditioning while waiting out the unbearable heat? So we succumbed again. In true vagabond style, we rinsed off a bit in the restrooms, bought a few cheap plastic, "made in China" storage bins for Charlotte, tried out a futon bed, sat on a bench, made some phone calls, and generally loitered.

By 5:30 we decided to take on the heat again, turning west onto Hwy 60. The bus was still running incredibly well, and it seemed that all the problems had dissolved as Charlotte got more enthusiastic about our road trip west. But then, 25 miles down the road, her exhaust became suddenly and dramatically…loud.

Ned looked in the rear view mirror in time to see the exhaust pipe rolling across the highway and drifting out of view. He quickly pulled over and looked under the bus. The entire exhaust system was gone, and flames were shooting directly from the number 3 cylinder toward the gas tank, posing an imminent fire (okay, explosion) danger. In all this time, we still had not been caught with our illegally missing registration, and had been lulled into a sense of placid security. I was, therefore, unprepared for the jolt of adrenaline as Ned decided to go ahead and back up the quarter mile to the last "farm" we had seen. Surely, if the cops didn't get us now, the explosion would!

We made it, but the "farm" turned out to be a series of three low, ramshackle buildings in a row, with absolutely no one around. Except the turkeys. Really hot, miserable, white turkeys, crammed into the ugly sheds by the thousands, covered with flies by the millions. There were so many of them that they could hardly move around. But they weren't caged, and even had a few watering devices scattered around. So, of course, we deduced that we had come upon a "free-range, cage free" turkey farm.

Ned pulled up next to one of the buildings and said he was going to hike up the road in search of our wayward exhaust pipe. The smell was horrible, and upon closer inspection, the poor creatures were actually panting in the steamy heat. Even worse, there were several 50 gallon barrels scattered around, filled with the rotting carcasses of the (lucky?) ones that didn't make it. So, with nothing better to do than keep Charlotte and the turkeys (dead and alive) company, I opened up a beer, sprawled out on the bed, swatted at flies, and listened to the sound of miserable, panting, "free-range" turkeys.

Ned returned shortly, exhaust pipe in hand, and proceeded to disable the number 3 cylinder so we would not explode. Car Whisperers really are handy to have around, but I have to say, Ned was discouraged this time. He explained that the pipe had rusted off right at the head and there was no way to reattach it. It looked like this might really be the end of the road. We shared gloomy visions of flying home and driving back with a tow rig, or of having to beg Leonard for a pre-Tetons rescue.

With heavy hearts we turned back east and limped on three cylinders toward Lake Crystal, a decent sized town Ned had noticed along the way. Our hope was to find someone in Lake Crystal who might offer some miraculous solution. However, on the way I saw a sign pointing to a town called Madelia. I suddenly got an eerily good feeling about it and urged Ned to pull off. Amazingly, he did, in spite of it looking like a tiny, two-horse farming town.

The little town did have a big roadside BP/Subway/AmericInn complex, and Ned went to consult the yellow pages inside the convenience store, while I ran to check out the AmericInn. By now it was around 7:00pm and raining again. I must have looked rather drenched and pathetic because the nice clerk, Jackie, offered me a 15% discount. It was the seventh night of our journey, and we *still* weren't camping, but the alternative was hanging out in the rain, and I was resigned and tired and it did look like a very nice motel.

I booked the room and went back to the convenience store. Ned was still pouring over the yellow pages, searching for auto repair places. But there was not much in Madelia. We doggedly decided that perhaps a welder would do or that we needed to find a handy farmer or something.

As we flipped through the phone book looking under "welders," we heard a squeaky teenaged voice behind us ask, "Do you folks need some help?" We whipped around to find a very large, pimply-faced "farmboy" standing there in his overalls with an equally strapping, pimply-faced friend hovering behind him. Ned asked him if he knew anything about welding, and he said, "Yup." "How 'bout Volkswagens?" Ned asked. "Yup." And just like that, they led Ned off to fix our Charlotte in spite of his doubts about her "fixability."

I escaped to the AmericInn, and, holed up in my fine motel room, I ate some food, called my Mom, and picked up a copy of the Madelia, Minnesota Visitors Guide. Madelia, *"The Pride of the*

Prairie," I discovered, is a grand town with a population of 2,307 and is located in Watonwan County. Watonwan has more than 240,000 acres planted in crops (mostly corn and soybean) yielding annual revenues in excess of $60 million. Madelia is also home to Down Foods, which is the largest producer of canned chicken (what, not turkey???) in the United States. I was also impressed to learn about the many clubs and service organizations one could join in Madelia. For instance, you could be a Boy Scout, or a member of the American Legion and Auxiliary, Rotary, or Lions Clubs. You could also join the Snowmobile Club, the Garden Club, the Saddle Club, or the Horseshoes Club...and if none of those appeal, you could always turn to Alcoholics Anonymous. I was sorry to learn, however, that we had just missed the annual Madelia Park Days, boasting a Carnival and Midway, a Hog Roast, a Church Bake Sale, a Burnout Competition, a Horseshoe Competition, and loads of exciting music and entertainment.

Okay, I admit to some "tongue in cheek" reporting here, but this really was a wonderful, wholesome little town, and when Ned finally got back to the room at midnight, I was even more impressed. Following my odd hunch had paid off. "Darren" and his friend turned out to be 17 years old. They had taken Ned and Charlotte back to the family farm where they ingenuously provided our "miracle" fix. Ned said that they immediately took charge and figured out a way to get the pipe back on the head. Darren had told his friend, "Remember that pipe over in the junk pile, the one about 'yay' big? Go and fetch it, would ya?" Then they proceeded to cut a piece off the scrap pipe and weld it into the hole in the head where the exhaust should come out, leaving enough on the other end to weld into the rusted, crumbling exhaust pipe. As Darren thought, it was a perfect fit, and a perfect fix, one that not even the Car Whisperer had thought of. Of course, that is typical of farmers, self reliant and resourceful because they have to be.

Darren and his friend had also noticed the Four Wheeler license plate and were bowled over to find out that Ned was THE Ned

Bacon, famous freelance writer. They invited a few friends over and had quite the little gathering. In the end, Ned gave them $100 to split, which they really appreciated (and did not expect) and we left Madelia with warm feelings and an operable bus.

Ned under the bus (a common sight) near the "free range" turkey farm.

Darren under the bus at his family's farm.

Chapter Nine

The Wild, Wild West

We got an 8:30am start on Tuesday, day eight. By the time we crossed the South Dakota border it was pouring rain again, they were predicting penny-sized hail, and we were enduring nasty bites from flies still hitchhiking from the turkey farm. But at least it was cooler, and the bus was running well. It was clear now that Charlotte was enjoying her first big adventure. She was cruising along perfectly at 60mph, so we figured were going to start having a little fun too. We were even cautiously optimistic that we would finally be able to camp that night.

Back on Hwy 90, our first (elective) side trip was to the Corn Palace in Mitchell, South Dakota. We had been seeing signs for it over the last 50 miles and figured it was just another bad tourist trap. We told our friends later that we only stopped because we needed to use the restroom, but I can admit now to a bit of curiosity. Well, no kidding, the place was pretty cool. It was a "palace" made of different colored ears of corn. The first one was built in 1892 as an entertainment hall and was rebuilt three more times (I guess the corn eventually rots). We were visiting the 2000 incarnation, and they still held concerts there. We played tourist for a while, then had lunch in the bus in the parking lot.

The Corn Palace in Mitchell, South Dakota. And yes, it really *is* made out of corn, lots and lots of different colored ears of corn.

Forty miles down the road, we pulled into Kimball, SD for fuel and followed some homemade signs away from the highway advertising cheaper gas. We pulled into the nicely rural (run-down) gas station only to find a police car sitting there. The cop had been chatting with the guy inside, but on his way out to his car, stopped again to talk with another fellow...right in front of our duct-taped, drooping headlight and bashed in front end. Uh oh...can't get out of Kimball??? But luck was with us again as he drove off without giving us a second look. We then pumped the gas before noticing the sign that said no bathrooms or credit cards, and Ned had given all his cash to Darren. Fortunately, there was an ATM inside, so we went in and had a chat with the owner, a big, friendly, robust, 65ish South Dakotan. He told us it was 117 degrees yesterday and 123 last week. We asked him how cold it got in the winter, and he drawled, "20 below usually, and sometimes 80 below with the wind chill. But it's ok, it's what keeps us healthy (he was born and raised there). The extremes make you healthy, and you just have to dress for it. You know, fur lined boots and gloves and insulated cover-alls." "In fact," he continued happily, "I once survived 24 hours stuck in a car at 95 below before being dug out of a berm." Yup, South Dakotans are way tougher than me.

On our way back to the highway, we saw the Doo-Wah-Ditty Diner. We stopped to use the restrooms, but couldn't pass up a chance for cherry pie and coffee. The sign on the wall read: "The best darn food you've ever eaten anywhere or we'll apologize, take your money anyway, and try to do better next time." How can you not love America's heartland?

We finally paid our National Park fee and drove into the Badlands at 5:30pm. The Pinnacles were spectacular, especially with the setting sun lighting up the dramatically banded colors of the peaks. Charlie's paintings had captured them well. It was getting late, but we managed to have some fun hiking around the nooks, peaks and gullies. We saw mountain goats and deer, and even had a close encounter with a buffalo. We especially enjoyed the absolute quiet of a place that was absent of human noise. As darkness came on, we were getting more and more excited to be spending our first night in the bus (if nothing else went wrong!).

We drove to an area in the park called Sage Creek, and were delighted to find that we could just pull over and spend the night. Not only were we actually *camping*, but it was *free*, too! Life was *really* good.

The Pinnacles in the Badlands National Park , South Dakota...spectacular, and well worth a visit!

It was slightly disappointing to not be able to camp in the Pinnacles themselves, but it was peaceful on the wide open prairie, Charlotte was cozy and comfortable, and our donated foam mattress was a dream. We went to sleep with smiles on our faces, and got a blissful night's sleep in our new "home."

Prior to departure the next morning, we were heralded along a leisurely hike on some buffalo trails by the famous "barking" prairie dogs. There were thousands of them, and they really were noisy little things. We even came across the first porcupine we had ever seen. It was huge, and, sadly, dead, but at least we could get a (safe) up close look! Pretty cool looking creature.

Charlotte's first dirt road was actually a wrong turn (20 miles each way) on our way to Mt. Rushmore. It was a happy accident, though, since it led us to a cute little Indian town called Buffalo Gap, and Charlotte got to get her shoes dirty for 40 miles. I could swear she was grinning.

A Badlands buffalo leisurely cruised in front of us as we headed for Sage Creek
and our first night camping!

Hwy 16 to Mt. Rushmore was one of the coolest roads we had ever been on. It corkscrewed sharply through a rocky, mountainous pine forest, through one-way stone tunnels and under massive, hand carved, wooden bridges…reminiscent of Thunder Mountain at Disney land, but much better! This was the famous Pigtail Bridges road in the Black Hills, and it was truly beautiful.

In general, Ned and I lean more toward "off-the-beaten-path" adventures, but the trend since Niagara Falls seemed to be, "oh well, we're here, let's see it!" We could not quite get into full tourist-mode, however, so in typical Ned and Kat style, we parked Charlotte way down the road and sneaked in cross-county to see Mt. Rushmore without paying. I supposed we ought to be ashamed of ourselves, but really we only stayed long enough to say, "Well, that's pretty impressive!"

Charlotte at Mt. Rushmore.

Okay, saw that, now on to the Crazy Horse Monument. Well, they wanted a fee there too! But the nice man at the booth, while laughing at our "thriftiness," was happy to hand us a brochure and point out that we could pretty much see it all from the parking area, albeit at a distance. We parked Charlotte just right so we could crawl in the back, eat some lunch, read the brochure, and look out at that wonderful work-in-progress. Evidently the huge monument is being carved from living stone, but has not been completed yet. And yes, that was impressive, too. And yes, we were loving "bus living."

The Wyoming border found us hungry, so we stopped at the Historic (touristy) Virginian Restaurant in the Occidental Hotel in Buffalo. The place was overpriced and full of tourists on cell phones, but the food was okay, and heck, this was our one and only "beaten-path" trip anyway!

We took Hwy 16 on into the Big Horn National Forest where we could find a place to sleep. National forests are wonderful because, unlike parks, you can pretty much sleep anywhere you can drive to. Ned and I like that kind of freedom. So it was, that Charlotte got her first real off-road adventure. We followed a steep, unmarked logging road up to a ridge, and she did great in 4-

wheel drive. Charlotte was finally getting a taste of what her new life would really be like! The ridgeline was open, due to a previous fire, so we were able to watch the moon rise as we played cards and got to sleep early.

A spectacular sunrise woke us early on Thursday, day ten. Stretching languorously like two contented cats while being treated to a gorgeous alpine view of the Big Horn National Forest, we were able to get a good 7:00am start.

Hwy 20 led us into the town of Thermopolis WY, famous for its free, state-run bath house. Evidently, the "World's Largest Hot Springs" used to belong to the Indians in the area, but they gave it over to the state with the promise that there would never be a charge for its use. We really liked that part. It was a beautiful, clean facility with a nice hot pool *and showers!* We were enjoying a delightfully peaceful soak when an older, rancher-looking man joined us and started talking. Now normally, we would love the opportunity to chat with a local Wyoming rancher, but this guy turned out, unbelievably, to be a white supremacist. No joking...he actually said that a good old-fashioned monarchy would solve all of our problems here in the United States, and that maybe Hitler was onto something! I crept over to the other side of the pool, leaving poor Ned to endure his odious ranting. Ironically, we later noticed that the nickname for Wyoming is "The Equality State."

Hwy 20 out of Thermopolis follows the Wind River and had the odd impression of traveling downhill, while the river was flowing uphill. We decided to leave it as one of life's little mysteries and drove on.

We had lunch in the Cowboy Café in Dubois. We wondered if a mid-Wyoming town would really sport a French name, so we asked the waitress, and she proudly told us that it was pronounced *"Doo-boys!"* Well, now, that makes more sense.

After lunch, we were back on the road, starting to feel really comfortable with our trip, when we suddenly encountered some road construction...and a cop pulled over just ahead of us. We were first in line approaching the flag-person, and Ned attempted to "get in line" behind the cop. Unfortunately, the flag-person and the cop both waved us up to the front so that our Four Wheeler Placard was right in the officer's face. "Dixie," the flag-person turned out to have a good sense of humor, so we told her the deal with our (lack of) license plates. She just laughed and said that there was an accident up the road and that the cop was probably preoccupied. She was right, and went on to tell us that she had been on this tedious, hot assignment now for five weeks. We couldn't help thinking back to our last five weeks...vintage auto racing in Seattle, a weekend House Party at some friends' beautiful "Blue Hole" in Grass Valley, CA, jeeping on the Rubicon Trail, and now, day ten of "Saving Charlotte," while Dixie stood in the hot sun and dealt with what she called "disobedient" drivers. We suddenly felt very humbled, blessed and grateful.

After crossing the Continental Divide over a 9,600ft pass, we went on to get our first glimpse of the "Tetons." The spectacular, "sawtooth" granite peaks soared to over 14,000ft and reminded us of the Mt. Whitney area off of Hwy 395 in California. The Grand Tetons are, of course, another National Park, but the Park Headquarters were located in town...the famous Jackson (Hole), Wyoming. We found Jackson to be quaint, if a bit pretentious, but the intern at the park, Emily, was enthusiastic and encouraged us to stay overnight and make the strenuous 16 mile hike to Static Peak the next day.

Our first gorgeous view of the Tetons as we headed for Jackson, Wyoming.

By now, we needed to re-provision, so we stocked up at the local grocery store, and then found an unpretentious place called "Bubbas" to get some dinner. The 30 minute wait found us hanging out in Charlotte, having a beer and reading the local paper. The editor was commenting on the recent heat wave (yeah, we know!) and quoting a New York woman who railed against the heat, crying, "It's unbearable, it's oppressive! My son couldn't even go to day camp because the air conditioning on the bus went out!" We laughed over the implication that "someone" should do "something" about it, and agreed that a lot of Americans could use a little "third-world travel" perspective.

"Bubbas" was great. The young waiter was polite, efficient, and energetic, and the shared, $14.95 "Mixed Grill" was perfect.

The wind picked up as we drove around looking for a place to stay the night, and by the time we (illegally) parked in a Trail Head parking lot an hour later, a storm had hit in full force. The wind furiously blew sheets of rain sideways at Charlotte's windows, thunder boomed ominously overhead, and lightning streaked the night sky. But we were warm and dry in our "Magic Bus," and, best of all, the chances of a park ranger driving by in the storm to kick us out were pretty slim. Bus living was even more wonderful than we thought!

We awoke the next morning to the wonderful feeling of sunshine peeking through Charlotte's windows, delighted that the weather had cleared for our big hike. We paid our $25 tribute to the National Park system and made our way to the Death Canyon trail head. Ned cooked us a hearty, bacon and egg breakfast, musing sadly that it was now Friday, day eleven, and this was the first time we had used the 100lb "cook box" we had been hauling around since we left Minden, Nevada. Motels, restaurants, and National Parks....perhaps it was best to get Charlotte used to her new life slowly. We certainly had great plans to make her into a capable off-road vehicle and show her what our kind of travel was really like.

The air was warm and humid after last night's storm, and the scenery along the trail was beautiful. We climbed 5,000 vertical feet, through pristine alpine forests with gorgeous displays of rushing streams, waterfalls, wildflowers, and lush green foliage.

We arrived at the top of Static Peak (11,300ft) and gazed around in awe. The sheer cliffs and majestic peaks of the Teton Mountains surrounded us like proud sentinels, and the backside of Static Peak dropped 1,000 feet straight down to a turquoise lake and glacier. We were well rewarded for our $25 entrance fee and 5,000 ft climb.

Half way back down the trail, the wind picked up and storm clouds began to gather again. The temperature was dropping quickly, too, but I couldn't resist the opportunity to challenge Ned to a nice dip. We had decided to have a snack beside a pretty little creek, and there just happened to be a perfect swimming hole...right there. So I stripped down and jumped in. It was, of course, ice melt-off, and the sheer cold left me gasping. I probably only immersed myself for about 2½ seconds, but the damage was done...now Ned had to get in too!

We declined a night on the town in Jackson in favor of a Charlotte "grazing" session and the chance to make it a little farther down the road. We happily drank a beer and munched on tuna salad, tomatoes, Greek olives, hardboiled eggs, and Swiss cheese while another lightning storm raged outside.

Starting up the 5,000 ft. climb to Static Peak.

Static Peak Divide at 10,790 ft. From there, we decided to go off-trail and climb to the top of Static Peak.

Ned dangles his feet over a sheer 1,000 ft. drop. Well rewarded for our 5,000 ft. climb…the airy views from the top of Static Peak at 11,300 ft. were incredible.

Not quite as brave as Ned, I sit a bit farther from the cliff ledge!

Charlotte had a hard time making it over the steep Teton Pass as we headed out on Hwy 22 and into Idaho, but she did it (at 25mph in 2nd gear!). Dark was coming on fast, but we were in Forest Service land, so a place to stay would not be an issue. We found a spot, read Alexander the Great for 10 minutes and contentedly fell asleep. We awoke to find ourselves in a lovely forest glade next to a stream, and got a good 7:00am start (after going back the ½ mile to snap a picture of the "Welcome to Idaho" sign!).

Idaho was uneventful, but we did enjoy the surprise view at Idaho Falls as the flat plains gave way suddenly to the huge, sheer walled gorge and Falls. Farther on, at Rogerson, we turned southwest onto a very cool back road, coming to another, even better surprise. Salmon Falls Creek was another canyon suddenly appearing out of the plains, and the road went over a very old, very leaky dam. The walls were steep, and the gorge was deep, so it was worthwhile to get out and take a look.

Off the beaten path in southern Idaho, we ran into Salmon Falls Dam. Deep, steep, old, and leaky, it was a cool surprise on our way to Nevada.

The road followed the canyon along a clean-running, lively little creek, and finally, at mile-marker 107, turned to *dirt*! We were now in our version of heaven; our confidence in Charlotte was growing, we had finally crossed the last state line and were happily tooling along off-the-pavement in beautiful Nevada. Our plan was to go through the town of Jarbidge and then all the way out to Elko ... 75 miles of remote dirt roads!

Crossing over....leaving the pavement behind for the next 75 miles. Yippee!

Feeling great to have left the pavement behind, but a little grimy again, I spotted a sign pointing to a place called Murphy's Hot Springs. I thought this might be a good place to get another bath, but it turned out to be a funny little two-dog town (both of them leashed to a tree). It looked like it was once a nice resort, but the cabins were all boarded up, and the place looked deserted.

The best way to cross state lines...on dirt! Charlotte makes it to her new home state of Nevada.

There was certainly no sign of any hot springs, so we moved on down the road.

We meandered along a beautiful, rock-walled canyon, still following the clear water stream, and just as it started raining, I spotted an old wooden bridge. I decided that I really did need a bath, so I asked Ned to pull over so I could go wash in the creek. It was cold and refreshing, but Ned was relieved that I did not press our reciprocity pact, stating that he was enjoying his "good crust."

Jarbidge had a good crust too. Well known as an outdoorsman's paradise, it was a very cool, no-pavement-in-sight hamlet, with two bars, a post office, and a scattering of funky old cabin-like houses. We parked under a sign heralding, "Booze, Grub, and Rooms," and went into the bar...where we were greeted by a crusty old bartender. "Don" was a little standoffish at first, but when we asked him to tell us about the "Shovel Brigade," he smiled, showing us his one tooth, pulled up a stool and said, "Well now, that's a great story!" Ned had been to Jarbidge before and knew a little about what had happened, but we got some great details from Don. It turned out that, because of the endangered Bull Trout, the Forest Service had closed (and partly destroyed) the southbound road to Elko, effectively boxing in the residents of Jarbidge. The locals organized a day to rebuild it, and folks came by busloads from as far away as Maine. In all, 3,000 outraged people showed up for what became known as the "Shovel Brigade." We were relieved to hear that the road was open now, but Don told us that it was still an ongoing legal battle. Don also told us that the town was named after a "giant, cannibal Indian."

Charlotte getting a taste of beautiful Nevada scenery.

There was only a scattering of locals in the bar when we showed up, but a few hunters on ATV's eventually started wandering in. We had a nice chat with a big Viking-looking guy from Elko, who ran a bulldozer at a mine, and we eventually had everyone in the place laughing as we regaled them with our "Charlotte" stories.

It happened to be "Prime Rib Night," at the Booze, Grub, and Rooms, so we "moseyed" into the restaurant and sat down, of course, right next to the local sheriff!

In all, we spent four hours in Jarbidge, enjoying colorful characters, good stories, and a prime rib dinner complete with apple pie and homemade ice cream (which the sweet, tattooed and pierced waitress had just made).

The town of Jarbidge, named after a "giant, cannibal, Indian, had a good crust too.

The now infamous road out of Jarbidge climbed sharply out of the canyon, and Ned eventually turned up an obscure side road to camp for the night. This was Charlotte's first real "hill climb," and she chugged right up the steep, gravely track. At 9,000 ft. elevation, we found a (rare) flat spot with a spectacular vista and "high-fived" each other. The weather was warm and balmy and both the moon and our bellies were full. We fell asleep again to more Alexander the Great, and woke to discover that this place was magical in its pristine beauty. Set beneath a backdrop of tall, granite mountains, the surrounding hillsides were lush and green, beautifully carpeted with bright purple flowers. Stands of aspen and pine were scattered around creating a truly majestic setting.

Further exploration rewarded us with more of nature's stunning art. The emerald hills rolled gently down into the canyon to the north, then stretched into the endless mountains to the south. Once again, we experienced the absolute quiet of far-off places, and left there with mixed emotions. We were glad to have camped in such a perfect spot for what had been the last night of our "Charlotte" trip, but we were a little sad, too, to have it all come to an end.

In the mountains outside of Jarbidge, at 9,000 ft. elevation, we were treated to a campsite with truly magnificent vistas. It was a perfect spot for our bitter-sweet, final night.

Charlotte sees more "real Nevada" on the way to Elko.

Chapter Ten

Charlotte Gets Us Home

We hit the pavement in Elko, and headed for home on Sunday, day thirteen. The only hitch in Charlotte's otherwise stellar performance was an attempt to head northwest, out of Winnemucca, back onto dirt roads, and on into the Black Rock Desert for one more camping night at our favorite hot springs. We were tempted to indulge her, but knew we had to get home to prepare for our next (this time jeeping) adventure on Thursday.

Civilization always feels like a sensory assault after time spend on back roads, and the drive home left us quiet and melancholy, enduring the trucks and traffic once again, and feeling a little let down after the last two exciting weeks.

But we began planning our next big bus adventures…what a wonderful way to explore the back roads, quirky places and people that make up the "real America." And of course, there was our beloved Baja, Mexico, the place where this whole idea was born, and where Charlotte was most excited to go.

Charlotte valiantly brought us home without so much as a hiccup since Madelia.
She did her job, now it was our turn to do ours. The repairs and upgrades
were well deserved.

In the meantime, however, there was much work to be done to make Charlotte more trail-worthy. In addition to repairing the crumpled front end, we had to replace her whole exhaust system, all of the hoses, do an oil change and tune-up, build front and rear bumpers to hold the winch, spare tire, gas can, recovery gear, and of course, bikes. She also needed a roof rack to hold the kayaks, a lift, new, bigger tires and wheels, a beefier engine, a new front (differential) locker, and a repair to the non-functioning, factory installed rear one. We also had to track down whatever issue kept popping up for the first part of the trip, to make sure it didn't happen again. It was a little overwhelming, but fortunately it's what Ned does and loves. He is, after all, The Car Whisperer.

We didn't know what to expect when we left home and more than once it looked like we might have had to abort the trip altogether. But Charlotte tugged at our heart strings, inspiring us to forge ahead, ignoring our extreme doubts about her road worthiness and lack of legality. There were times of uncertainty, times of physical discomfort, a few adrenaline rushes, and even a couple of "spats." But we never lost confidence in each other and came home with a sense of real accomplishment and camaraderie.

68

We were proud of our new "Magic Bus," who left the East Coast, struggling and dragging her tires with apprehension, but who never really "stranded" us, nor even ever stalled. Charlotte was excited now to have a new life. We were excited to have Charlotte.

Epilogue

Baja at Last

It's Christmas Eve, 2007, and we are dreamily laying in our bed in Charlotte on the beach at Gonzaga Bay, Baja....our favorite place in the world. The waves are gently lapping on the shore of the Sea of Cortez, and dolphins had, earlier, been playing in the beautiful sunset waters. A gentle rain has started pattering on the roof, and we smiled at each other, thinking how wonderful it was to have come full circle. No, we were not watching an off-road race in the rain this time, but we were sitting on the beach in the rain, having a lot more fun. We were on a three week, back roads of Baja trek, with six other VW Syncros, and it was just the beginning of the adventure. Charlotte is hardly recognizable in her new "bad" off-road get-up. Ned has done an amazing job, and she is performing spectacularly.

Together, we lay there and reminisced about the trips we had made in the bus so far. We had gone on a 14 day, 1,400 mile, all dirt Nevada adventure (Charlotte finally got to the Black Rock Hot Springs!) and we even took her to Easter Jeep Week in Moab, UT where she got called "The Toaster," on the technical "slick rock" trails. There were also countless other, very comfortable, overnight and weekend trips to various places, and we were still loving this particular mode of travel.

We also reminisced about the day we first arrived home with her. Strangely, Charlotte pulled into the driveway without so much as a hiccup, but when we took her to get the mail the next morning, she would not run. The same issue that had us nearly crippled for the first part of our homeward journey was back. Charlotte had valiantly brought us home, mysteriously overriding what turned out to be a common Vanagon quirk, requiring an expensive replacement part. We will never understand how or why she got us so far, but it certainly added to her charm. By saving Charlotte we had rescued a bus with real soul.

Baja at last!

Afterword, by Ned Bacon

Technical Stuff
and Special Friends

Kat asked me to write about all the "special stuff" I've done to Charlotte since our fateful trip across the country back in "06. I must admit that I didn't know a lot about VW Vanagon Syncro mechanics and their idiosyncrasies before buying Charlotte. But one learns fast, or else sits alongside the road when relying on these things for transportation!

After we arrived home from our inaugural cross-country trip, I went to the Internet for information. I soon found the GoWesty website and a cornucopia of answers to questions I was asking. S. Lucas Valdes, the owner of GoWesty, has written a library of answers to frequently asked questions and frequently experienced problems relating to life with a Vanagon. His business in Los Osos, CA specializes in all things Vanagon, and especially, all things Syncro. Lucas and his right-hand-man, Taylor, the general manager of GoWesty, are into Syncros for the same reasons I am: we want to four wheel them where no one would dream of taking them, and live out of them while we are doing it.

My first phone call to GoWesty after I purchased Charlotte was answered by Taylor. He quickly explained the quirks relating to the Bosch Digifant Intake Air Sensor and the subsequent drivability problems associated with it – the exact problems Kat and I had experienced during the first half of our trip. One rebuilt

Intake Air Sensor later and Go Westy had a new customer. I had found my first true soul mates in "The World According to VW Syncros."

Since that first phone call I have literally rebuilt our Syncro mechanically from front to back, utilizing GoWesty's vast resource of parts and knowledge. The extended GoWesty crew and their families have all become good friends of ours, to the point where we've shared great trips in Baja together. Once you are into one of these vans they truly become a member of the family, and like any family member, 'ya love 'em despite their quirky ways.

The following is a list, from the ground up, of all the modifications I've performed on Charlotte since installing that first (of three) Intake Air Sensors:

- TIRES   Currently rolling on B. F. Goodrich KM Mud Terrains 30 – 9.50 X 15s.

- WHEELS   15 X 7 rims welded with stock VW Vanagon centers. Custom built by Stockton Wheel. Late '60s VW Bug hubcaps.

- BRAKES   Front: Stock Discs   Rear: Heavy Duty South African Vanagon Drums.

- FRONT SUSPENSION   Owner reinforced lower control arms, H&R coil springs (GoWesty) Fox 2.5 Remote Reservoir Shocks with owner built custom shock mounts, Light Racing Jounce Shocks. GoWesty upper ball joint spacers. Approximately 3.5 inches of lift over stock.

- FRONT DIFF.   GoWesty European sourced housing with factory locker. 5.43 ring and pinion. Viscous Coupling removed and replaced with solid shaft.

- FRONT DRIVE AXLES   Stock

- STEERING Stock

- DRIVESHAFT Stock

- REAR SUSPENSION H&R coil springs, Fox 2.5 Remote Reservoir Shocks. Approximately 3 inches of lift over stock.

- REAR DRIVE AXLES Sway-A-Way (GoWesty) 'shafts with Porsche 930 CV joints

- TRANSMISSION original case rebuilt by GoWesty with taller 1.18 3rd gear and .77 4th gear. Front axle Decoupler.

- REAR DIFF. 5.43 ring and pinion with factory locker

- ENGINE GoWesty 2500cc stroker Waterboxer (up from stock 2.1 liter) Makes 125hp and 175ft/lbs (up from 96hp and 116ft/lbs stock) BIG DIFFERENCE! Stock fuel injection and ignition. 160 amp Delco alternator (part of Premier Power Welder onboard welder). Old AC compressor converted to onboard air compressor for tire inflation.

- CLUTCH Kennedy Stage II

- BUMPERS owner built front and rear. Front holds a Warn 9000# winch with Masterpull synthetic rope and two Light Force HID driving lights. Rear features owner designed swing out spare tire carrier with 7 gallon extra gas can. A Pull Pal portable winch anchor mounts to bumper. 2 inch receiver hitch with Warn "D" shackle.

- SKIDPLATES 3/16 inch 6061 T6 aluminum front and rear. Front protects from bumper to back of front diff. Rear covers all of trans and engine/exhaust

- BODY original burgundy paint. All doors, panels and glass original (except windshield) Right front corner bash was repaired with a big hammer and a gallon can of Bondo. Pre 1986 front grill installed with 7 inch round headlights (IPF H4 halogens with 90/145 bulbs) Rattle can flat black paint job on dent area.

- INTERIOR – FRONT original driver's and passenger seats. Passenger's has a 180 swivel. Dash is original with a Sony CD stereo with MP3 (4 speakers) Lowrance Baja Pro 540 GPS is mounted in old ash tray hole. CB radio is overhead in ex AC vent tube. Inoperable AC was removed and old overhead ducting was converted into storage for books, maps, towels, etc.

- INTERIOR – REAR 6 foot Minneapolis built bed with 4 inch foam still workin'. Down comforter with flannel sheets. GoWesty storage nets on rear windows. All rear glass is "limo tinted" so no need for curtains. ARB fridge/freezer, Rubbermaid cook box (pots, pans. Coleman stove, BBQ, utensils, seasonings, cups, plates, propane bottles, etc) 4 foot folding cook table, 5 gallon portable water tank. Persian rug. (Every hippy bus has gotta have one) Under bed: 2 camp chairs, tools and recovery gear, huge deep cycle marine battery, spare parts and fluids.

- ROOF 2 Thule roof racks for kayaks, BP solar panel.

Not your average "hippy bus!" Charlotte having a good romp in the Black
Rock Desert

The Black Rock Hot Springs!

Ned entertains me and Charlotte while camping at the Hot Springs.

The vast, wide open beauty of Nevada.

Long abandoned mining shacks in remote Nevada.

Looking out from what was once a family's dream home.

On the west side of the Ruby Mountains in Northern Nevada, we found a very remote track to cross over to the east side. We come across this historic Pony Express Trail marker at the summit.

A room with a view! The first thing we saw waking up in the Ruby Mountains.

We hauled kayaks around for 1,400 miles of Nevada's remote dirt roads and finally had our one and only chance to paddle.

The Ancient Bristlecone Pines in the White Mountains outside of Bishop, California. These trees thrive at 11,000ft. elevation and were saplings when Abraham roamed the earth 5,000 years ago!

Romping and playing in our own backyard.

The famous Hole in the Rock in the Grand Staircase Escalante National Monument. This is where the Mormons lowered wagons on ropes down a steep cliff in order to cross the Colorado River (before it was dammed to create Lake Powell).

A camping night to remember in the Escalante National Monument!

We were told that this remote dirt road out of the Escalante National Monument was impassible because of wash-outs, so of course, we took it anyway! We were rewarded with some incredible scenery.

Coming out the other side of the "impassible road"...no sweat for Charlotte!

Yum! A typical camp dinner.

Nothing like cooking up some bacon and eggs on the edge of a 1,000 ft vertical drop! We found this cool canyon coming out of the Escalante on our way to the Arizona border (on dirt roads, of course!).

Another perfect camping spot in the San Juan Mountains in Colorado.
Charlotte had just spent the day climbing over several of the gorgeous
12,000 to 13,000 ft. passes.

Is this really Baja, Mexico??? Yes, it is…in the mountains of Northern
Baja near Laguna Hansen.

Charlotte sure brings us to some cool places. We were in Southern Baja
along the Sea of Cortez searching for some elusive hot springs.

Roaming Baja with our GoWesty friends.

The Sea of Cortez. Charlotte was the only Vanagon on the trip that was not a Westfalia Camper.

Crossing Baja from the Sea of Cortez to the Pacific Ocean.

Kat Wicchert, a self-proclaimed "desert rat" with "itchy feet," lives in Northern Nevada, but has a hard time staying put. She and Ned Bacon share a mutual wanderlust and enjoy hiking, skiing, trail running, mountain bike riding, jeeping and adventure travel both here in the United States and in exotic countries around the world. Whether backpacking the Inca Trail to Machu Picchu, enduring a 30 hour rickety train ride in Viet  Nam, desert racing 1,100 miles in a Jeep in Baja, Mexico, or just crossing Nevada on dirt roads in "Charlotte," Kat is happiest in motion.

Kat holds a BS in Business Administration from UC Berkeley and is a Posture Alignment Specialist and Personal Trainer. She is the President of Ever Active, Inc. and owns the Pain Free Posture Nevada studio in Minden, NV. Kat is passionate about fitness and, when not enjoying far-flung adventures, helps her clients attain more rewarding lifestyles by improving their physical capabilities.

CPSIA information can be obtained at www.ICGtesting.com
Printed in the USA
LVOW010530290812

296406LV00007B/94/P